THE JOY OF RUGBY

THE JOY OF RUGBY

Summersdale Publishers Ltd
46 West Street
Chichester
West Sussex
PO19 1RP
UK

www.summersdale.com

Printed and bound in the Czech Republic

ISBN: 978-1-84953-601-1

Substantial discounts on bulk quantities of Summersdale books are available to corporations, professional associations and other organisations. For details contact Nicky Douglas by telephone: +44 (0) 1243 756902, fax: +44 (0) 1243 786300 or email: nicky@summersdale.com.

THE JOY OF RUGBY

STEVEN GAUGE

summersdale

DEDICATION

I'd like to dedicate this book to my delightful offspring Ellie and Dexter Gauge, who have both now discovered some of the joys of rugby for themselves, and to their mother and my wife, Sue, for her phenomenal patience and tolerance as I have been enjoying this sport and its associated activities rather extensively (particularly with Warlingham Rugby Club) over the years.

CONTENTS

INTRODUCTION

When Mrs Webb Ellis lost her husband at the Battle of Albuera in 1811, during the Peninsular War, she decided to move to Rugby in Warwickshire. This allowed her two sons, William and Thomas, to take advantage of a free education at Rugby School, offered to boys living within 10 miles of the school clock tower. Her decision, combined with William's apparent inclination to 'take unfair advantage at football', has given us a wonderful game that is now played in over 100 countries around the world.

According to a letter written in 1880 from Matthew Bloxam to *The Meteor*, the Rugby School magazine, William Webb

Ellis caught the ball during a game of football in the later half of 1823 and, instead of retiring back down the pitch and kicking the ball as the rules then required, he 'rushed forwards with the ball in his hands towards the opposite goal'. Today there is a bronze statue beside the school and a plaque on a wall commemorating Webb Ellis and describing how the young man 'with a fine disregard for the rules of football as played in his time first took the ball in his arms and ran with it thus originating the distinctive feature of the rugby game'.

There is something about the phrase 'with a fine disregard for the rules' that for me captures the joy and spirit of rugby.

One can easily imagine a predictable kick-around on a wet Wednesday afternoon in Warwickshire being brought to life by a spirited young chap deciding that the game would be a whole lot more interesting if the players could make use of all four limbs. The thought that, rather than punishing or suppressing this burst of youthful exuberance, Webb Ellis's peers decided to play along with him, creating a new game, is delightfully uplifting and life-affirming.

It's not only the rules that get treated with a fine disregard, of course. Rugby breeds a certain sort of player who will throw his or her whole body into the game with fine disregard for personal safety, decorum or dignity. Once a week, rugby allows people to test themselves physically by launching into huge tackles, diving into great heaving, rolling mauls and unleashing powerful runs through determined defences – all in the interests of carrying an odd-shaped ball over a white line painted on the grass. I don't know if that's quite what Webb Ellis originally had in mind, but therein lies some of the joy of rugby.

There is also something deeply joyous about a game that brings together towns, cities, regions and nations to cheer on the finest players of rugby and share with them every impact, every kick and every scrum. Whether watching a local club in a lowly league from the touchline, or an international fixture from one of the world's great stadiums, the collective experience, the shared humour and the sheer pleasure of watching the sport is much the same.

You can turn up to many a rugby club on a Sunday morning and see hundreds of children from aged five to 18 discovering the joy of rugby. They might start off with the contact-free, tag and touch version of the game, saving nervous parents from premature grey hairs and intermittent heart failure. After a few years, however, they are desperate to try tackling, scrummaging, rucking and mauling as they grow in confidence, stature and strength. On a cold, muddy weekend you cannot force anyone to play rugby; they would only do it if they loved the game.

Some of us come to rugby later in life. I only really discovered the game at the age of 35 and found a sport that was, to my surprise and delight, more than welcoming to someone of my age and with my lack of discernible talent. In clubs all over, third-, fourth- and fifth-team captains will warmly embrace anyone new who wants to try out the game. With larger bodies finding a home in the forwards and thinner, faster types free to run around in the backs, joy flows from rugby's ability to find a place on the pitch for almost anyone.

Even after the final whistle has blown, the joy of rugby continues. The feeling as you walk off the pitch after a game, and shake hands warmly with the same people who only a few minutes earlier you were trying to tear down to the ground, is a mixture of relief, exhaustion and contentment. There is a sense that you have been through a very raw and whole-hearted primal experience, and that you have very much earned the beer that awaits you in the clubhouse bar.

Rugby, it turns out, is more than just a game; it is a celebration of what we can achieve physically as individuals, together as a team and a club, and sometimes, as those World Cup competitions come around every four years, as a nation. So whether you play the game, watch the game or are just trying to fathom why so many other people do, sit back and enjoy these chapters of celebration of the mighty sport that is rugby. With a fine disregard for whatever else it is you are supposed to be doing today, share with us now a little of the joy of rugby.

HOW IT ALL STARTED

Forasmuch as there is great noise in the city caused by hustling over large balls, from which many evils may arise, which God forbid, we command and forbid on behalf of the king, on pain of imprisonment, such game to be used in the city in future.

PROCLAMATION FROM EDWARD II, 1314

Long before the day when William Webb Ellis picked up the ball at an elite public school, there were plenty of common folk enjoying the simple pleasure of throwing a ball around in a competitive fashion. In medieval Britain, villages staged games where huge mobs would compete to carry an inflated pig's bladder from one side of the town to another.

The purest form of the game survives today in places like Ashbourne in Derbyshire where, every Shrove Tuesday 'Up'ards' (those born north of the River Henmore) compete against 'Down'ards' (those born on the southern side) to get a ball from the car park in the centre of the town to one of two mills on the outskirts. There are few rules and the game can last for up to eight hours, but if no one has scored a goal by 10 p.m. the ball must be returned to the Green Man and Black's Head public house for safekeeping until the following year.

The Irish had a game called 'caid' involving two large teams, a leather-clad, inflated pig's bladder and quite a lot of physical contact. With the huge quantities of beer that were also consumed, it wasn't just the pig who got bladdered. The Welsh version was called 'cnapan' and would pit sides with up to 1,000 players against each other. In France, in spite of the best efforts of the religious authorities, a game called 'la soule' was played with a leather ball filled with hay, bran or horsehair.

In New Zealand, long before the Europeans put in an appearance, the Maoris played a game called 'ki-o-rahi' involving two teams competing on a circular pitch. The game is played with a small ball, called a 'ki', made from woven flax. This ancient fibrous plant material also seems to have helped to weave together the DNA that later would form the all-conquering All Blacks.

The Kiwis traditionally held a gathering of the players called a 'tatu' before each game of ki-o-rahi to agree the rules that would be applied. The English, being English, opted for a series of committee meetings with formal agenda, apologies for absence and detailed minutes. In 1845 three boys at Rugby School got together and duly produced the first printed set of rules. Later in 1871, three lawyers, who also happened to be old boys from Rugby School, drew up the laws of the game. These laws were swiftly adopted by the Rugby Football Union.

Let the games begin

 Rugby clubs had been formed as the boys from the school moved and entered employment. While Webb Ellis became a vicar, some of his contemporaries joined the medical profession and the first rugby club to get itself organised enough to have an inaugural annual general meeting was at Guy's Hospital in London. No doubt the injuries thus sustained gave them some useful subjects to practise upon as they honed their surgical skills.

In 1857 former Rugby School pupil William Mather put together a side made up of his old schoolmates, and invited an old schoolfriend and school captain to bring over a similar side from Manchester. An exhibition game was played in front of a large crowd at Liverpool Cricket Ground and the groundsman marked out the pitch using white chalk. Clubs were formed in Liverpool and Manchester as a result, and pioneering rugby player Richard Sykes went on to take the game to the USA, where the first rugby clubs were formed in the San Francisco Bay Area in 1872.

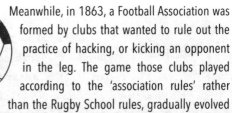

Meanwhile, in 1863, a Football Association was formed by clubs that wanted to rule out the practice of hacking, or kicking an opponent in the leg. The game those clubs played according to the 'association rules' rather than the Rugby School rules, gradually evolved into the game that involves kicking a more strictly spherical ball, marrying pop stars and models, and regularly delivering theatrical performances towards the referee complaining that your opponent has kicked you in the shin. This game was hereafter known by most people as football, by Americans as soccer and by rugby pedants as 'the association game'.

The first international test

The first rugby international fixture was between Scotland and England in Edinburgh in 1871. The catalyst for the fixture was a somewhat irascible Scottish reaction to having been defeated in a football international the year earlier, disputing the lineage and heritage of some of the players who had been assembled to represent their nation. The Scots claimed that rugby football was the preferred game north of the border and so challenged the English to put together a side. Twenty English players were assembled, including John Clayton from the Liverpool club.

Did you know?

John Clayton's training regime for the first-ever international rugby fixture consisted of a 4-mile run every day for a month with his large Newfoundland dog acting as pacemaker and personal trainer.

With 13 forwards on each side, the game turned largely into an extended maul with the backs rarely getting a look-in. In those days points were awarded solely for kicking the ball through the goalposts, either from a drop kick or from a converted try. There were no points for touching the ball down over the line, an achievement which simply qualified the side for a 'try' at kicking for goal.

Early in the second half of the game the Scottish forwards managed to push an extended scrum over the English try line, and Angus Buchanan grounded the ball, claiming the first-ever international rugby try. The dispute that followed, however, set the tone for the treatment of match officials by players to this day.

Referees were not introduced into the game until a few years later and so an umpire observing proceedings from the touchline resolved any disputes. The umpire, a well-respected local headmaster called Dr Hely Hutchinson Almond, was subjected to a barrage of protestations from both sides and was called upon to decide whether the try should stand.

Having no idea whether the try had been correctly obtained or not, he confessed afterwards,

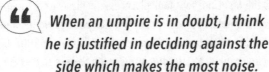

When an umpire is in doubt, I think he is justified in deciding against the side which makes the most noise. They are probably in the wrong.

The English players were the loudest, so Scotland were awarded the try and William Cross kicked the conversion (another first for international rugby), securing the only points of the game. To this day rugby players are much more likely to quietly accept a referee's decision, unlike those who play with the round ball.

The game on tour

One of the delights of the game today is how well it lends itself to a tour, when a side packs its bags, kisses its loved ones goodbye and settles in for an extended trip filled with rugby, good humour and beer. As English Victorian gentlemen travelled and settled around the world, taking the game with them, very soon overseas tours became a possibility.

In 1888 the first Lions tour took place, essentially as a ruse to get some cricket promoters out of a spot of financial bother. Two separate teams of English cricketers had been touring Australia in 1887–88 and had nearly bankrupted the organisers in the process. Rather than give up, go home and face their creditors, the organisers hatched a plan to put together a rugby tour given they had already invested quite a lot of money in getting Down Under, and establishing contacts with the different sports clubs and municipal authorities. They also tried to persuade some of the cricketers to stay on and play some rugby before going home.

Twenty-two additional players were recruited from back home, mostly from northern clubs, but also including a handful from Wales and Scotland. After sailing for six weeks on a boat from Gravesend they met up with the tour organisers in Port Chalmers and began a series of 35 games in New Zealand and Australia – of which they lost only two. They even tried their hand at a spot of Aussie rules football, winning seven games and drawing in three.

The Lions' penchant for hard drinking clearly began with this tour. The two Scottish tourists Dr John Smith and Dr Herbert Brooks were both reported by Charlie Mathers, who kept a diary of the tour, to have played rugby while intoxicated. Brooks reported more euphemistically that throughout the tour the team had received a 'hearty' reception wherever they went.

Tragically, halfway through the tour they lost their captain Robert Seddon when he was killed in a boating accident on the Hunter River in West Maitland, New South Wales. He was buried in West Maitland in his flannel trousers and rugby top in the Campbells Hill Cemetery, after a procession led by 180 local players and the mayor and aldermen of the town.

When the tourists returned to England on 11 November after eight months abroad, the different nations had all learnt new things about the game from each other, and the Lions had established a relationship with rugby fans in the southern hemisphere that would see the tours continue throughout the following century and will no doubt go on through the next.

Gilbert – a rugby brand with an impressive heritage

William Gilbert owned a shoe- and boot-making business located close to Rugby School. He turned his hand to making rugby balls for the boys following these, now obsolete, steps:

Step 1: Take one pig's bladder still in its fresh, smelly, 'green' state.

Step 2: Inflate the pig's bladder using a clay pipe and human lung power. Try not to inhale as the pig's bladder may well be infected.

Step 3: Stitch together four leather panels using a waxed thread, stitching inside out to begin with.

Step 4: Wrap the leather panels around the bladder, and finish off the stitching with a new thread.

Gilbert's nephew James gained a reputation among the pupils at Rugby School as being 'a wonder of lung strength and blew even the big match balls up tight'.

Their effort clearly paid off. Gilbert's early rugby balls were displayed and won medals at the Great Exhibition in 1851 and the Great London Exposition of 1862. The ball changed shape over the years as the game evolved, becoming smaller and more pointed. In 1890 the first laws were introduced governing the size and shape of the ball and today the Gilbert brand adorns the official match ball of the Rugby World Cup.

CHAPTER 2

ONE GAME, TWO CODES

I'm 49, I've had a brain haemorrhage and a triple bypass and I could still go out and play a reasonable game of rugby union. But I wouldn't last 30 seconds in rugby league.

GRAHAM LOWE, FORMER NEW ZEALAND RUGBY LEAGUE COACH

Charles Darwin published his *On the Origin of Species* in 1859 with his theories of natural selection. It had taken a sober and academic tour of the Galápagos Islands and the surrounding area to gather the evidence to support his theories of adaptation and survival. However, he could have stayed at home, had a beer or two and observed the evolution of two very distinct sub-species of *Homo rugbyus*. The sport of rugby in the north of England was having to adapt to a different economic environment, and was about to branch off and give birth to an entirely new variety of the game – rugby league.

Towards the end of the nineteenth century rugby was becoming hugely popular in northern cities, with vast crowds paying to watch teams compete. The clubs were generating substantial revenues, but none of it was allowed to find its way into the players' wallets as a code of amateurism was strictly enforced by the game's regulators.

The players, mostly drawn from traditional working-class trades, would also struggle to earn a living if they were injured in the course of a game. A proposal was put to the Rugby Football Union to allow clubs to pay players for 'broken time', to compensate them for any time missed from work.

The RFU had been formed by public school boys, many of whom didn't have to worry about maintaining a steady income. The RFU, dominated by southern clubs with their aristocratic and aspirational middle-class members, voted down the proposal and northern clubs were suspended if they were suspected of paying players.

In August 1895, 21 clubs met in the George Hotel in Huddersfield and, after three hours of private deliberation, resolved to form a breakaway Northern Rugby Football Union specifically to permit the payment of players for broken time. The game played from then on in the northern leagues became known as rugby league, and the game played under the auspices of the original RFU became known as rugby union.

A different league

The two branches of the game evolved and developed in their own different ways. In rugby league, the game became much more open as the scrum stopped being a monumental battle to see which pack could push the other off the ball. Instead, it has become a device for tying up a few players in the centre of the pitch to give the others in the team a little more room to run around. Each tackle in rugby league is ended when the attacking player is deemed by the referee to have been held.

With paying crowds to entertain and salaries to pay, rugby league needed to be open and entertaining, with everyone able to see the game. Rugby union on the other hand, remaining a strictly amateur sport, retained rucks, mauls and scrums, where the so-called dark arts of forward play are largely hidden from the spectators' view.

Rugby union remained an amateur pursuit for the next hundred years. During that time, no rugby league player was ever allowed to play rugby union; while rugby union players were banned from ever playing rugby union again if they were tempted to switch codes and play the northern game.

Leagues apart - the differences between the two codes

	Number of players per team	What happens after a player is brought down in a tackle	Scrums
League	13	Tackled player is allowed to stand up and heel the ball back to a teammate to restart the game.	Two packs of six players each are formed. There is no real pushing and the side putting the ball into the scrum always gets possession.
Union	15	The tackled player has to release the ball. The tackler has to roll away. Other players compete for the ball and a ruck is often formed.	Two packs of eight players are formed. The ball is meant to be placed strictly in the middle of the scrum and both sides will push and compete for the ball.

Ball goes into touch	Points for a try	Points for a drop goal	Points for a penalty
Restart with a scrum.	4	1	2
Restart with a line-out, where the ball is thrown in between two lines of opposing forwards.	5	3	3

In the early 1900s, clubs in the southwest of England attempted to form a western branch of the northern union. Numerous clubs and players were banned, including one James Peters, who had been the first black man to play rugby union for England.

Peters played for England against Scotland and France, and had thoroughly irritated a touring side from apartheid South Africa when he appeared in the line-up for a Devon RFC side that the South Africans were due to play. The South African High Commissioner had to persuade his fellow countrymen to take to the field as he feared a riot from the impatient crowd. Peters was, however, left out of the England squad that played South Africa later in the tour, purely on racial grounds.

Peters was not to play another game for England and was later suspended for accepting payment from Devon RFC. He headed north and saw out his career playing rugby league for Barrow-in-Furness and then St Helens, before retiring from the game altogether in 1914.

Fortunately, the two codes have now pretty much buried the hatchet and permit players to transfer between rugby league and rugby union. Some great players, such as Jonathan Davies and Jason Robinson, have now played both codes, and both versions of the game have almost certainly benefited as a result. Robinson was one of the first to switch to rugby union having made his name in the Wigan Challenge Cup-winning side. Nicknamed Billy Whizz, he played in 56 union internationals and scored 30 tries, including one in England's World Cup victory over Australia in 2003.

Converts from league are now regularly welcomed into the union fold. Andy Farrell made the switch from league in 2005 and now coaches the England backs, including his son, the fly half Owen Farrell.

For many years rugby union struggled to hold on to its amateur status. At the top level players were expected to make a substantial commitment to keeping fit, training and playing; senior players could see fellow sportsmen and women earning a respectable living in other games.

Some have argued that turning a blind eye to some of the payments to Welsh players prevented the growth of rugby league on the other side of Offa's Dyke. When the Welsh international Arthur Gould was awarded the deeds to his house in 1897, the RFU declared him a professional and banned all clubs and players from playing with him. Only when the Welsh Rugby Union withdrew from the international board and began making moves to join the NRFU was a 'compromise' reached and those blind eyes were turned.

As rugby union grew in popularity during the 1980s and more money found its way into the sport, clubs found a range of ways to get around the rules and compensate their players:

Being given a not-too-arduous 'job' by a generous club benefactor with a big business, which allowed extensive periods of absence for training and fixtures.

Being employed by the club as a 'coach' or 'groundsman' with no real duties other than training.

Being paid for personal appearances by corporate entertainment types.

Giving in and finally going off to play rugby league.

Being paid for endorsing products. Boot money – whereby players would find some cash rolled up in their boots in the changing rooms.

Fifty-seven old farts

Players and regulators were often at loggerheads over their interpretation of the laws about what they could and could not be paid for. Matters came to a head in 1995, when in a TV interview in the build-up to the World Cup that year, England captain Will Carling publicly and memorably attacked the people who were in charge of the game, saying,

> **If the game is run properly as a professional game, you do not need 57 old farts running rugby.**

The old-fart-in-chief at the time was RFU secretary Dudley Wood, who had adjudicated disputes over payments for personal appearances and product endorsements, including one case of £100 in Burton clothing vouchers, which were awarded to Simon Hodgkinson for winning a Player of Merit contest.

The old farts were the 57 members of the council of the RFU, who govern the game, drawn from the constituent bodies that make up the rugby union, including representatives from each county, along with the Army, Royal Navy and Royal Air Force's rugby sides. After a good deal of harrumphing, the decision was made to allow players to be paid to play and the character of the game at a senior level changed forever.

... Or did it?

The spirit of amateurism still lives on in the vast majority of clubs around the world. In England the old farts are still in charge, although now there are around 60 of them. A few were added to represent players and referees, and there is one to represent women and girls.

In 2011 a lengthy report was commissioned from the leading international law firm Slaughter and May, which concluded that the way rugby was administered could perhaps be a little more efficient. The old farts fought back; and after an 18-month consultation period, the sport's rulers concluded that, mostly, the sport should stay more or less as it is.

For all the frustrations and limitations of its old-fashioned nature, there is something quite heart-warming about the way rugby is run in England. In spite of the sport being a huge business, with TV revenues swelling the coffers of the leading clubs, it remains a game that is effectively owned and democratically controlled by elected representatives of all the clubs, down to those in the very lowest leagues or those merely playing occasional games against casual sides. Anyone with a real love of the game and enough time on their hands could one day find themselves being a club chairman. Once you have done that it is only a short jump on to a county committee and, before you know it, you too could become an old fart on the RFU council and have a say in the way rugby develops and changes in the future.

Now we are 61

At the end of 2013 there were 61 members filling 62 positions on the RFU council, including former England captain Phil Vickery and his former teammates Jason Leonard and Richard Hill.

35 REPRESENTING THE CONSTITUENT BODIES (28 COUNTIES, WITH THE LARGER ONES HAVING MORE THAN ONE REPRESENTATIVE)

7 REPRESENTING SCHOOLS

4 PRESIDENTIAL ROLES

3 FROM THE ARMED FORCES

2 INTERNATIONAL RUGBY BOARD

2 NATIONAL

1 CO-OPTED

1 REPRESENTING REFEREES

1 REPRESENTING THE PLAYERS

1 MORE TO REPRESENT WOMEN AND GIRLS

1 CHAIRMAN

1 CHIEF EXECUTIVE

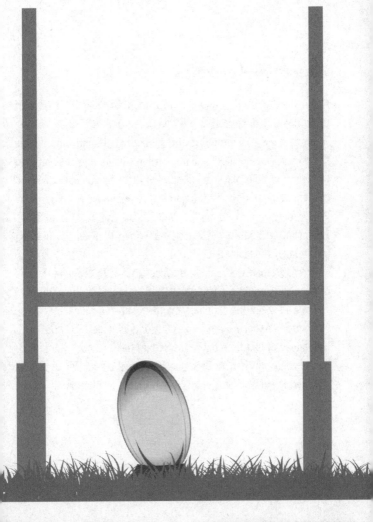

The cross-code challenge

As relations thawed between rugby union and league, a clash of the codes was organised in 1996 between Bath RFC, that season's winners of the Pilkington Cup and the Courage League, and Wigan, the previous season's RFL Championship title-holders. Played over two legs, the sides played a full game of rugby league at Old Trafford in Manchester and then a full game of rugby union at Twickenham. With two tries from Martin 'Chariots' Offiah and more from Jason Robinson, Scott Quinnell and others, Wigan finished the first leg comfortably ahead at 82–6.

Two and a half weeks later, the sides met at Twickenham for the rugby union leg. In the first half Wigan struggled in the eight-man scrum and conceded a penalty try for collapsing repeatedly. Bath, with international players Mike Catt and Phil de Glanville, were well ahead at half time but in the second half the sides were much more evenly matched. As Bath began to tire, the fitter Wigan players matched them point for point. They scored two phenomenal tries, which both started from behind their own try line, Jason Robinson demonstrating the blistering pace that earned him the nickname Billy Whizz. The game ended with Bath the winners, but by a closer margin of 44–17.

Jason Robinson would subsequently transfer from league to union and would win 51 union caps for England to add to his collection of 12 union caps for Great Britain and seven for England. Scott Quinnell, who had switched codes two years earlier leaving Llanelli RFC to join Wigan, switched back to union in 1996, joining Richmond, and played in the Welsh side that reached the World Cup quarter-finals in 1999.

CHAPTER 3

PICK YOUR OWN POSITION

The appeal of rugby for the player is that it is designed to cater for men of any physique as long as they have that vital fire which is worth a ton of theory.

BOB STUART, ALL BLACKS CAPTAIN

One of the many reasons why rugby is such a great team game is that it celebrates and capitalises on our differences, finding the perfect role for everyone. We come in a wide range of bizarre shapes and sizes but for every single one there is a perfect position on the rugby pitch. Different personalities may thrive in different places, too. Every role in a rugby team has its own particular pleasures, as the following diagram is designed to illustrate.

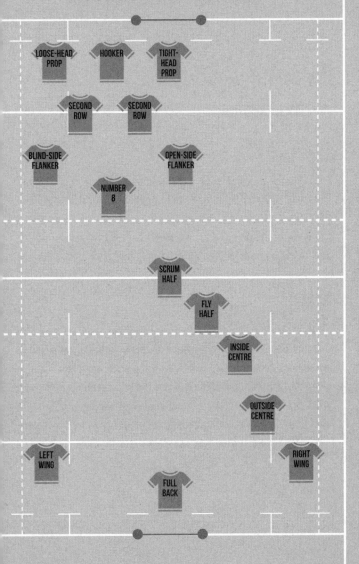

RUGBY UNION POSITIONS

LOOSE-HEAD PROP

HOOKER

TIGHT-HEAD PROP

SECOND ROW

SECOND ROW

BLIND-SIDE FLANKER

OPEN-SIDE FLANKER

NUMBER 8

SCRUM HALF

FLY HALF

INSIDE CENTRE

OUTSIDE CENTRE

LEFT WING

RIGHT WING

FULL BACK

The joy of being a...

Prop

Props are the two players on either side of the front row of a scrum. The joy of this position is in the pure battle of physical strength and technique with the opposite number. Props are also allowed to eat a few more of the pies and are excused from running-around duties, as a little extra body weight is important in those front-row battles.

Hooker

Hookers play in the middle of the front row of the scrum and have the pleasure of pretty much guaranteed contact with the ball, as it is their job to hook it back from the middle of the scrum. Hookers are also given the task of throwing the ball in at the line-out and can, over the years, gradually earn respect from their teammates for simply being able to throw the ball in a reasonably straight line at a convenient height for a pre-arranged member of your team to catch.

Second-row lock

Players in this position can bask in the glory of being the 'powerhouse' of the scrum. A lock's job is to push the props forward in the scrum with their shoulders and lock out their legs to prevent the props from being pushed backwards. Partially because of where the locks are expected to put their heads, squashed between the backsides of the hooker and the props, they will also be more likely than many other players to acquire the ultimate rugby status symbol, a cauliflower ear.

Did you know?

Cauliflower ear, or hematoma auris, is caused when the ear is hit and a blood clot collects between the cartilage and the other layers around it. The cartilage then dies, forms fibrous tissue and the outer ear becomes permanently deformed. Psychiatrists in the 1800s thought it was linked to insanity. Some rugby players refuse to have it treated and regard it as a badge of honour.

Flanker

The great thing about this position is that flankers are able to get out of the scrum first, avoiding any unpleasant pile-ups, as they only really need to hang loosely to one side or the other. As a result flankers will also often be the first forward to get to the ball or to get to an opponent with the ball – so if you enjoy running with the ball or tackling anyone else with it, this is almost definitely the place to be.

Number 8

This is the position right at the back of the scrum usually reserved for the most experienced and capable of all the forwards. The number 8 is the only player who is allowed to break off from the scrum and pick up the ball and run with it. Alternatively they can choose to allow the backs to have the ball if they prefer. Number 8 is pretty much in charge and everyone knows it.

Scrum half

The joy of being a scrum half is getting to boss all the forwards around in spite of being approximately half their size. The scrum half's job is to lurk behind the forwards, trying to keep out of trouble and extracting the ball once in a while to give to the backs. A scrum half needs to be brave, fearless and able to pass quickly and accurately to the...

Fly half (or a bit stand-offish)

One of the glamorous positions, the fly half is able to enjoy the game without worrying too much about whether it might mess up their hair. The backs might not get the ball too often from the forwards, especially on a wet muddy pitch, but when they do, it is up to the fly half to decide what to do with it. They can kick for distance and get the team out of trouble in defence, or set up a clever running move with the rest of the backs. The fly half calls the moves and is the envy of all the other backs.

Centre

There is much fun to be had here either tackling, or shimmying and sidestepping with the ball through the opposition's attempts at tackles, setting up and occasionally even scoring tries. Typically centres will be the finer physical specimens of the backs and most of their game is in the open periods of play. A centre's efforts will be seen and appreciated by any spectators who happen to be around.

There are two centres, an inside centre and an outside centre, but that doesn't mean that one of them conducts the entire game from within the clubhouse. The inside centre is the one closest to the fly half, probably the more senior of the two and the one most likely to be flattened when an attacking move goes wrong.

Winger

The wing is a great place for a player carrying less weight, who can therefore run a little quicker than their teammates. On the wing they can keep well out of trouble for much of the game and, very occasionally, when the ball has been through everyone else, will find themselves with the ball in their hands and a very short distance to run and score a try.

Full back

Before retiring from the game everyone should play here at least once. This position is the last line of defence and, although that can be a little nerve-racking, the full back is a total hero if they make a try-saving tackle. They will also be under a lot of high kicks and, if they can catch it without dropping it, will have the opportunity to have a nice long run with the ball before anyone can attempt to stop them.

Meanwhile in rugby league...

In rugby league there are only 13 players on the pitch, so there is a little more multi-tasking and the players tend to be a little more alike and interchangeable. Rugby league teams seem to have come to an arrangement that means there is rarely any real pushing in the scrums, so the bulk of the forwards are much less important. Instead, everyone in a rugby league side needs to be lean, strong, fit and fast.

The positions are much the same as in rugby union but without the two flankers. Forwards are still expected to be the strongest players, able to break through tackles and make important hard yards up the pitch. Backs are expected to be a little quicker, more nimble and able to make the final breakthrough to score tries.

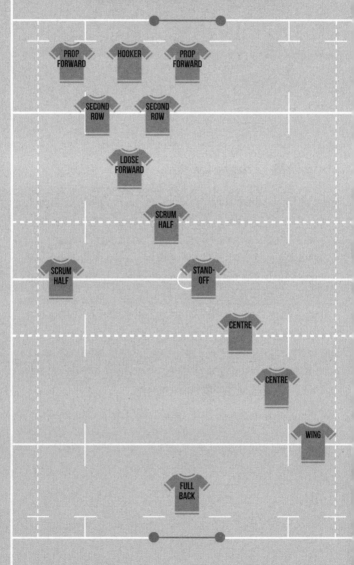

RUGBY LEAGUE POSITIONS

PROP FORWARD

HOOKER

PROP FORWARD

SECOND ROW

SECOND ROW

LOOSE FORWARD

SCRUM HALF

SCRUM HALF

STAND-OFF

CENTRE

CENTRE

WING

FULL BACK

The joy of being a...

Dummy half

After a tackle, the person being tackled is allowed to get up and heel the ball back to a teammate to continue the play. The player who picks up the ball is called the dummy half and anyone can have a go. It is typically the hooker's job, but if they are being tackled then someone else will step in.

Scrum half

This position in league is actually a little more like the fly half in union. The scrum half will be the player who receives the ball passed from behind each tackle and will determine, with the fly half, the way the game unfolds from there.

Old rugby players never die – they just change positions

Very few of us stay exactly the same shape and retain the same levels of physical fitness throughout our lives. Rugby turns out to be a remarkably accommodating sport and, as your body changes over time, so can your position. Many a young winger has, with the passage of years, acquired a few more muscles and perhaps a little more weight around the middle and found themselves in the front row at a later stage in their career. England hooker Tom Youngs started his rugby career as a centre before a coach at Leicester Tigers gently encouraged him to sample the delights to be found in the middle of the scrum. Many an amateur end-of-season tour fixture has involved players trying their hand at a new position just for fun and an additional challenge, and to see the game from a new perspective.

THE CLUBHOUSE

The spirit was excellent. Yes, we were all naked together at times, but so what? The only chaps who were perhaps a bit shy initially were those with small willies.

ANONYMOUS SOUTH AFRICAN RUGBY PLAYER COMMENTING ON THE 2003 WORLD CUP SQUAD TRAINING CAMP

Probably more than any other sport, rugby has developed an image that is just as much about how players socialise and celebrate as it is about how they play the game. Very few people would confidently predict the likely goings-on at a cycling or athletic club social gathering. Rugby clubs, on the other hand, have a bit of a reputation.

From the moment the referee blows the final whistle to when the bar manager calls last orders, rugby clubs still provide one of the most spirited, hearty and hospitable environments for players and spectators to recover, rehydrate and unwind after a game.

Ah yes, the bar. The place for a quiet pint followed, as former English international Gareth Chilcott once said, by 15 noisy ones. The songs and the antics that come after a game are tame compared with what might have just happened on the pitch, but they are all part of the joyful rugby experience. Keeping brewers in business while setting innuendo and double entendre to music, the rugby club bar can be a boisterous but utterly brilliant institution.

Sociologists and political theorists do rather fret about the decline in the numbers of people who are members of clubs and societies (something they call 'social capital'). Meanwhile, around the world and in the nation that gave birth to the game, rugby clubs continue to survive in good numbers and host some of the most spirited post-match celebrations and other social events imaginable.

The rise and rise of rugby clubs

Over the history of the game there have been a few particular periods when rugby clubs have significantly grown in strength and number. In the 1870s as the RFU was formed, the new association gave clubs an impetus to become constituted and acquire a clubhouse. In the 1920s club numbers increased again. Rugby became seen as a mark of middle-class respectability. The 'better' schools switched from the association game to rugby and their old boys formed new clubs when they left.

In the 1950s, improving economic conditions meant that rugby clubs had to compete with alternative leisure pursuits. Televised international fixtures led to fewer people watching local games from the touchlines. Clubs needed to improvise to survive as their revenues declined. In Wales, Llanharan RFC built changing rooms from surplus RAF units and some clubs pooled their clothing ration coupons in order to get enough kit to play in.

In the swinging 1960s, numbers surged again as rugby union became a little more democratic and spread further across society. Michael Green, author of the brilliant book *The Art of Coarse Rugby*, argues that rugby 'began to be discussed in workshops as well as board rooms… and few clubs bother about where a player went to school'.

Academic seal of approval for post-match celebrations

Today rugby still wins when it comes to socialising. A learned and academic report entitled 'Social and Economic Value of Sport in Ireland' by Tony Fahey and Liam Delaney of Ireland's Economic and Social Research Institute found that rugby generates the greatest frequency of socialising among players. Eighty-six per cent of Irish rugby players socialise with other rugby players at least once a week, and certainly more often than they socialise with university academics.

Rugby is a sociable game and, as it turns out, is good for your soul as well as keeping you fit. The same Irish report found that 'members of sports clubs report higher levels of physical and mental well-being throughout the life cycle than the rest of the population'. They concluded that sports club membership is part of a package that helps people live a healthier life and grow old more successfully than the rest of the population.

In 2003, rugby became Britain's second-most-popular sport after football, according to a national opinion poll, when 27 per cent of British adults expressed an interest in the sport. This might have had something to do with the success of the England team in winning the Rugby World Cup that year, but it meant that more than 15 million adults were now interested in rugby union. Rugby league came in eleventh in the same poll, while union's popularity had also spread beyond its traditionally white, male, middle-class audience, with interest increasing among women, the young and even a few people who had been educated in a comprehensive school.

Beer, beer and more beer

Where there are rugby players, there will be beer, and the success of rugby clubs has often been linked to healthy profits behind the bar. Rugby players are just as competitive off the pitch as they are on it, with almost as much kudos to be gained from winning a post-match drinking contest as there is from scoring a try mid-game.

After a few drinks, there are sometimes a few songs. Ideally these will have an easy-to-learn chorus and a few lewd and innuendo-laden verses for the more seasoned club members to perform. Songs are handed down from generation to generation and in less politically correct times songbooks and albums have been published to celebrate the genre of the rude rugby song.

And then there was more beer

Rugby players will often display a 'fine disregard' for the normal rules of social decorum. When the French President Georges Pompidou was making a speech at the post-match banquet after France had beaten Wales in 1973, the players persuaded the Dax town band to march in playing their instruments and bring the rather tedious oration to a premature end.

Elaborate games have been developed in rugby clubhouses solely for the purpose of encouraging more drinking. Traditionally a 'boat race' is held, where two teams of eight hardened drinkers line up against each other in an alcoholic relay; they then proceed to consume eight consecutive pints, upturning each empty glass on their own head just to prove that its contents has been consumed.

Tonbridge Juddians RFC claims to have introduced the Wibbly Wobbly game to Britain, where two teams line up and the players take it in turns to down a pint, run to a stump, place their head upon it and then circle it ten times before setting off back to their teammates. Tonbridge eventually had to ban the indoor version after one month of playing it resulted in more injuries than the team could sustain.

Games involving rules that become more incomprehensible as the evening wears on have evolved to trap the unwary into a desperately drunken evening. Fortunately for the players' livers and for the safety of the clubhouse fixtures and fittings, a greater adherence to drink-driving rules over recent decades has probably led to a decline in the greater excesses of rugby clubs. But beneath the surface of every rugby club lies a very messy evening just waiting to happen.

Tips for drinking a yard of ale

1. Don't!

2. If you must, start by handing over your car keys. You are not driving home today.

3. Remove as much clothing as you dare. There will be spillage, and your smart post-match shirt and club-tie outfit will be ruined.

4. You may well be required to stand on a chair. If so, make sure that there is plenty of headroom to lift up the yard glass high enough to empty it.

5. Take your time. Lawrence Hill of Bolton, Lancashire, features in the Guinness World Records for drinking a 2.5-pint yard of ale in 6.5 seconds in 1964. You are not going to beat that, so don't try.

6. Twist the glass as you drink. It evens up the air pressure more gradually and should stop all the beer from tipping out at once.

7. If there is a big surge of beer, don't widen your mouth to try and catch it. It will all end up coming out of your nose, eyes and possibly even your ears – and that won't be pleasant for anyone, least of all you.

8. That's it really. You then just have to drink it.

9. Take a bow and congratulate yourself for keeping your rugby club entertained.

CHAPTER 5

TACTICS
AND MOVES

*Rugby is a wonderful show: dance, opera and,
suddenly, the blood of a killing.*

RICHARD BURTON, ACTOR

Rugby is at its heart a fairly simple game, but the opportunities
to gain strategic advantage through intelligent game play are
practically endless. There is also a delicate interplay between the
tactics employed by the skilled player and the development of
the laws of the game. While coaches and captains will conspire to
contrive new ways of winning, the laws of the game are tweaked and
twiddled almost every year to refine the sporting spectacle and keep
people relatively safe.

Rugby has laws (drawn up by lawyers) as opposed to rules
(presumably made up by rulers or other items found in school
geometry sets), and they are designed to encourage a physical battle
to see which players can carry the ball furthest and fastest, and which
players are strong enough to stop them. The guiding principles in the
opening chapters of the International Rugby Board law book set out

how they attempt to balance the contradictions between encouraging players 'exerting extreme physical pressure' while making sure not to allow anyone to 'wilfully or maliciously inflict injury'.

All the laws seek to reward superior skill. So if one side kicks the ball out of play because they cannot see a way through to run it up the pitch, then the opposing side gets the advantage of the throw in at the line-out. If a player can't catch a pass and knocks the ball forwards, the opposing side has the advantage of their scrum half getting to put the ball into the middle of the scrum (the put-in).

The law about passing the ball backwards is a primary example of that principle in action. If for any reason a player doesn't feel brave enough or strong enough to carry the ball forwards and has to pass it, they have to pass it backwards. If you are not going to run forwards with the ball, you certainly can't move it forwards by flinging it up the field. You can save that sort of behaviour for netball.

The game, your fellow players, the supporters on the touchline, even William Webb Ellis watching from somewhere up above, are all willing you to run with the ball as hard as you can, only stopping to pass it to one of your teammates when there really is no alternative.

Keeping it interesting

There is one special law that when called upon can override all other laws in the interests of keeping the game interesting and entertaining. It's called the 'advantage law' and it means that referees can acknowledge but wilfully ignore any transgressions while waiting to see if the transgressed side can gain some sort of advantage without any help from the officials.

As the novelist and rugby union referee Derek Robinson said,

> **The advantage law is the best law in rugby, because it lets you ignore all the others for the good of the game.**

Once again the principle of 'fine disregard' is applied to increase the joy that is obtained from the opportunity to play the game.

Tactics

Rugby is of course more than just a battle of brute force. Obviously physical strength is important but an ability to make clever decisions can be just as influential in determining the outcome of any given game. A combination of a commanding physical presence, a degree of bravery and an ability to spot tactical opportunities in a fast-moving game makes for a great player. Two or three people like that on your side can make for a great game.

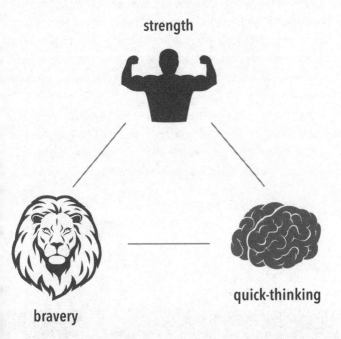

strength

bravery

quick-thinking

Tactics for forwards

Scrums

To the outside observer the scrum might not seem like a very tactical part of the game – a heap of players pack down together, the ball is popped into the middle and, after much huffing and puffing, the ball seems to pop out again somewhere else. The reality, as all forwards will tell you, is very different. Grouped under the heading 'the dark arts' are a number of micro-strategies available to the more advanced player.

With such great forces at work, a small adjustment in body position can make a huge difference in a scrum. When a front row is struggling, often the best response is for the props to try to be fractionally lower as the two packs engage. A lower body position enables the props to push up at a slightly different angle and gives them a marginal advantage.

A well-organised pack may also try to slightly wheel the scrum round, without the referee noticing, so that the whole team are in a better position when the ball comes out and the opposition's defenders are blocked from getting to the ball.

If things are going well in the scrum and you are not being pushed backwards there is also a tactical decision to make about how long to keep the ball in the scrum at the feet of the number 8. You might want to keep the ball in the scrum and push forwards a few yards, just to edge up the pitch a little, sapping the strength of your opposing pack. If things are not going so well, however, you want to get the ball out quickly, give it to the backs, and let them try to kick or run their way out of trouble.

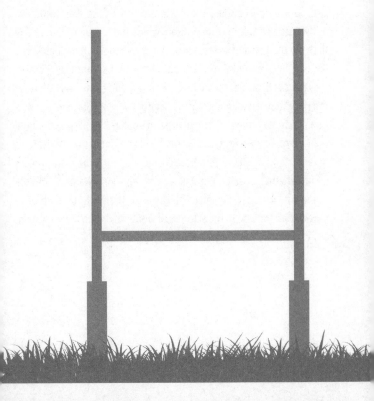

Line-outs

Line-outs are also packed with tactical choices. Each team will have its own set of codes to communicate where the hooker is going to try to throw the ball and what the catcher should do with the ball when they get it. A line-out throw that goes close to the front may increase the chances of a safe, secure catch, keeping possession and allowing the pack to make a little progress. Alternatively, if your hooker has a good accurate throwing arm, getting the ball to the back of the line-out, and more quickly across the park, will stretch out the opposition's defences and may give you more chances to score. There are choices about whether to catch the ball and for all the forwards to huddle round into an attacking maul, to drive up the pitch or whether to quickly flick the ball to the scrum half while still being held up in the air, 'off the top', enabling the backs to have a run.

The entire tactics of front-row play can be summed up in the following infographic, which has been drawn up in collaboration with some of the world's finest rugby strategists and sports scientists.

Forwards' tactics

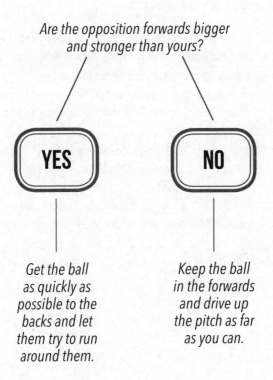

Are the opposition forwards bigger and stronger than yours?

YES

NO

Get the ball as quickly as possible to the backs and let them try to run around them.

Keep the ball in the forwards and drive up the pitch as far as you can.

Attacking moves for backs

The job of the backs is essentially to find gaps in the opposition defences and run through them carrying the ball. Their strategy and tactics are geared towards creating more of those gaps and getting their players into the right place at the right time to exploit them.

The tricks and techniques used in the forwards may be known as 'the dark arts', but for deception and deviousness you should look no further than the sorts of things the backs get up to as they seek a small advantage over their opposition. Backs' moves are filled with dummy passes and runners coming out of surprising positions at unusual angles. There are lots of histrionics, as centres, wingers and full backs attempt to trick the defenders into going in one direction as they set off in another. The side that is better at playing the theatrics and the mind games is more likely to get a breakthrough and a try-scoring opportunity.

A simple backs' move

In this move the full back joins the line of attackers giving them an extra man. As the ball gets to the outside centre the winger moves in closer to the centre, drawing in the opposition player marking him. The ball is then passed straight to the full back, who catches the ball while running at speed through the gap that has been created between the last defender and the touchline.

A more complicated backs' move

Here the ball is passed to the inside centre (number 12), who then turns around with his back to the opposition and shapes as if to make two dramatic dummy passes. The first is to the fly half, who is running around apparently to catch a loop pass. The second dummy pass is made in the direction of the outside centre (number 13), who is running through in the opposite direction. By this point the opposition defenders should have moved to where the dummy runners were heading and, with a bit of luck, left a gap for the blindside winger, who has run over from the other side of the pitch to exploit it.

There is, of course, plenty that can go wrong with any backs' move. Players have to time their runs absolutely perfectly so that when and if they do catch the ball they are in the right place and running at full speed. Dummy runs need to look convincing and are often accompanied by a large shout calling for the ball, but must not be so convincing that they confuse the player making the pass. Most importantly, everyone needs to remember the calls and codes and not make it completely obvious to the defenders what they are about to do.

Sadly, however, the lot of the back in rugby is not always a happy one. On a cold, windy and wet afternoon, in the middle of winter, it is quite common for long periods of the game to pass without the ball finding its way to the backs at all. The most frustrating thing as a backs player can be to spend the hour before the game rehearsing and perfecting a series of wonderful elaborate moves, only to find that once the game starts the forwards either refuse to give you the ball or, even worse, keep losing it to the opposition.

Defensive strategies for backs

In defence there are tactical choices to be made. At its simplest it often boils down to a choice between a 'drift' or a 'blitz' defence.

Drift defence

In a drift defence, the backs will try to shepherd the attacking side towards the touchline by pushing forwards on the inside shoulder of the attacking players and allowing the defensive line to be slightly sloped with the outside players hanging back. In a set-piece play from a scrum, it requires a little assistance from one of the flankers to put pressure on the attacking fly half, and that allows the defending side to drift across and gives them one extra defensive player.

Blitz defence

The blitz defence is a much more aggressive approach, as the name implies. The defending line rushes forwards as a straight line, putting pressure on all the attackers and often forcing them to make mistakes. It cuts down the time the attackers have to make decisions but at the same time it also commits defenders – which is fine if they are the sort of defenders who never miss a tackle, but it makes them vulnerable to an attacking side with a few moves of its own.

Game plan

Occasionally the forwards and the backs will agree a 'game plan', a broad agreement about how long the forwards will try to hang on to the ball before passing it out to the backs. Players will talk about one, two or three phases of attack where the forwards take the ball until they get stopped. Only then will the backs be given the ball and invited to run around. Game plans, however, very often go out of the window once the referee blows the whistle to start the game. Many a terrified forward will completely forget the strategy in the face of a ferocious onslaught from the opposition.

At different stages of the game you might see the forwards repeatedly picking up the ball from the back of a ruck, that wonderful name for a seemingly random heap of players piled on top of the ball, and running just a few feet into the next tackle. This can go on for some time as the attacking side attempts to draw in all the defending side's forwards, wearing them out, and perhaps forcing them to make a mistake and concede a penalty. Then, when the scrum half thinks the time has come and enough damage has been done, he or she will pass the ball out to the backs to exploit any space that has now been created.

THE GLOBAL GAME

I love rugby because it's a sociocultural experience; travelling the world and meeting people... actually it's more for the frequent flyer points.
JAMES HOLBECK, AUSTRALIAN RUGBY COACH AND FORMER PLAYER

For many casual supporters of the game, their experience of rugby is primarily an international one. The game reaches its widest audience around the times of international test matches and tours rather than club fixtures and national leagues. However, at every level of the game rugby feels like an international sport, with friendships and rivalries stretching all around the globe.

Playing teams from other countries and cultures is as much a part of the experience and joy of the game as the smell of Deep Heat in the changing room before a game or the drinking and singing afterwards. For many sides, from schoolboy teams to local community clubs, the international tours and exchanges often take on a far greater significance than any domestic competition.

The game has spread from its birthplace in England to all the continents (games have even been played between the research scientists of different nationalities at Scott Base in Antarctica), and every nation that picks up the oval ball adds a new dimension and spirit to the game. Here we take a look at the international characteristics of some of the different nations that play the game and the teams that represent them at the highest levels.

France

The British introduced the French to the game in the 1870s. In Le Havre, a group of British residents began playing a hybrid of football and rugby, and in 1877 a group of businessmen in Paris formed English Taylors RFC. Soon there were two Parisian teams, Racing Club de France and Stade Français, and by the time of the Paris Olympics in 1900 the French were sufficiently well organised to pick up the gold medal. Rugby is pretty much the dominant sport in the south of France, with almost all of the senior sides based in that region.

The French have a reputation for playing a rough, and some might say brutal, game in the forwards but combining it with a certain Gallic flair in the backs. Serge Blanco, their greatest-ever try-scorer described the game as 'just like love. You have to give before you can take. And when you have the ball it's just like making love – you must think of the other's pleasure before your own.'

The national side didn't really come into its own until the late 1950s and the French won the Five Nations tournament for the first time in 1959. Gloriously unpredictable, the French have made it to the World Cup final three times but have not yet managed to pick up the Webb Ellis Cup.

New Zealand

We have Christ's College in Finchley, north London, to thank for introducing New Zealand to the game of rugby. In 1867 the fee-paying boarding school welcomed a young Charles Monro from New Zealand and with a strict, highly disciplined regime began to prepare him for a military career. However, it also taught him the set of rules for football as played at Rugby School, and the young Monro played for the school's second team. When he returned to New Zealand in 1870 Monro set about convincing Nelson Football Club to try out the Rugby School rules. They played New Zealand's first rugby game on 14 May 1870 against Nelson College in front of a crowd of 200 spectators.

Old boys from English public schools established rugby clubs in Auckland, South Canterbury and Otago, and, helped by a thriving transport network and legislation that led to a growing practice of half-day working on Saturdays, the game quickly caught on throughout the provinces. When Auckland played Christchurch in 1875 there were 3,000 spectators.

Today the All Blacks are the most feared and respected international rugby union side with their motto 'Subdue and penetrate'. As the former Australian player Phil Kearns said,

> *You can go to the end of time, the last World Cup in the history of mankind and the All Blacks will be favourites for it.*

And yet they have, so far, only captured the top prize twice.

Papua New Guinea

When Australia took over administering Papua New Guinea after World War Two, the particular Australians that travelled there happened to take rugby league rather than union with them. By the 1960s the game had completely taken hold of the nation. With a population of just seven million, Papua New Guinea is the only nation to declare rugby league as its national sport. Matches in Papua New Guinea are a huge event and spectators have been known to walk for days in full tribal dress to attend fixtures.

There are 600 different languages spoken in Papua New Guinea and tribal disputes can occasionally make team management tricky. During one tour, the organisers had to work hard to keep the news from two players that their respective tribes had gone to war.

Close links have been formed between Papua New Guinea and the English rugby league side Hull Kingston Rovers. In 1996 Hull KR signed Papua New Guinean star John Okul and his friend Stanley Gene. Gene went on to coach at the Hull KR academy and Gateshead Thunder, as well as serving as head coach for his nation in 2010. There is a Facebook page linking supporters from Hull KR and those from Papua New Guinea, with supporters swapping team kit and news about their players through the social-media site.

South Africa

The highs and lows of rugby in South Africa have all been closely linked to global politics. The team's very first tour of the northern hemisphere in 1906 was an attempt to improve international relations following the Boer War. The sporting boycott during the 1980s reduced their national side, the Springboks, to playing matches against rebel tours.

In contrast to the isolation and hostility to South African rugby in those years, hosting the 1995 Rugby World Cup was one of the most uplifting and inclusive moments in post-apartheid South African history and international sport. Few will forget seeing President Nelson Mandela wearing the Springbok jersey, which up until that point had been seen as a symbol of white suppression in the country, as he handed the Webb Ellis Cup to captain Francois Pienaar.

Italy

Italy didn't play their first international game until 1929 when they lost 9–0 to Spain in Barcelona. After World War Two, allied troops in Italy helped to develop the game, and an assortment of foreign players and coaches continued to support rugby as it developed in the nation.

Known as 'the Azzurri', the Italian rugby team earned themselves a place in the Five Nations tournament in 2000, turning it into the imaginatively titled Six Nations. As the perennial underdogs of the competition they are many people's second-favourite team.

Italy won their first game in the Six Nations at home to Scotland, but it wasn't until 2007 that they managed to secure an away win when they defeated Scotland at Murrayfield by 37–17. They have qualified for every World Cup since the tournament was created in 1987 but are yet to progress beyond the group stages.

One of Italy's greatest stars played his first two international tests for Argentina, the country of his birth, but in 1991 Diego Domínguez returned to his mother's homeland and began playing for the Azzurri. Over a glorious career he won a further 73 caps and remains one of only five players in history (the others being Dan Carter, Jonny Wilkinson, Neil Jenkins and Ronan O'Gara) to score more than 1,000 international points.

Australia

Rugby began to be played in schools across Australia during the 1860s as teachers from England brought the Rugby School rules along with them. Scratch sides were occasionally assembled to play against visiting naval ships and by 1874 there were enough clubs to form the Southern Rugby Union, although initially it was administered from Twickenham in England. In 1892, the Southern Rugby Union became the New South Wales Rugby Union and administered the sport alongside the Queensland Rugby Union.

On their first tour to the northern hemisphere, some sections of the British press attempted to bestow the nickname of 'the rabbits' on the visiting side. The Australians were not keen to have their national side named after a species that had been imported from England and had become a pest. A vote among the tourists was arranged to select a more suitable animal and the native wallaby was duly elected.

The Wallabies became a dominant world force in the 1980s with an all-conquering tour to the British Isles in 1984. In 1999 they made history by being the first nation to win the Rugby World Cup twice, beating France in the final at the Millennium Stadium in Cardiff by 35–12.

Major international rugby tournaments

The Six Nations

This tournament started life as the Home Nations Championship in 1882, between England, Scotland, Wales and Ireland. France joined in 1910 and suggested renaming the tournament the Five Nations. Italy joined in 2000 and then there were six.

Teams play each other once only, alternating home and away over successive seasons. Two points are awarded for a win and one for a draw, and the side with the most points at the end wins the Championship Trophy, a sterling-silver trophy first presented in 1993.

For England, Scotland, Wales and Ireland, there is an honour to be won called the Triple Crown, awarded to the side that beats all the other home nations in a season. There wasn't a trophy to accompany this award until 2006 when the sponsors RBS organised a silver platter.

Any side that wins all of its games in one season can claim a Grand Slam. No physical trophy accompanies this one, but the team gets bucketloads of kudos. The side that finishes bottom of the table is awarded the wooden spoon, although no actual carved, cake-stirring implement is handed over.

There are a variety of trophies, real and imaginary, over the course of the tournament. Selected individual fixtures have their own trophies:

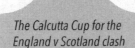

The Calcutta Cup for the England v Scotland clash

The Centenary Quaich for the Scotland v Ireland fixture

The Giuseppe Garibaldi Trophy for the France v Italy game

After that there are a variety of trophies depending on how many games you win.

The Rugby Championship

This is the southern hemisphere's equivalent of the Six Nations in which Australia, South Africa, New Zealand and Argentina compete. It was previously known as the Tri-Nations before Argentina joined in 2012. Inaugurated in 1996, the contest has been completely dominated by New Zealand, with the Kiwis winning 12 out of the first 18 competitions.

The teams play each other twice per season, home and away, and there are bonus points to encourage more tries and losing sides to hang on in there and keep the losing margin to seven points or fewer.

There are also individual fixture trophies within the tournament:

The Bledisloe Cup for the overall winner of the Australia v New Zealand games

The Freedom Cup for the victor of the fixtures between South Africa and New Zealand

The Mandela Challenge Plate for the best out of the Australia and South Africa games

The Puma Trophy, which would leave something for Argentina to win if only they could beat Australia.

The Rugby World Cup

The Rugby World Cup is a relative newcomer to the international sporting calendar but it already attracts the third-largest global audience for a sporting event. Although it was first mooted in the 1950s, it wasn't until the early 1980s that the Australian and New Zealand RFUs joined forces to put together a feasibility study.

On 21 March 1985 the committee of the International Rugby Board met in Paris to decide whether or not to go ahead with the idea. The home nations were opposed, fearing that it would inevitably become a huge commercial affair and undermine the game's amateur ideals. New Zealand, Australia and France were supportive, and when South Africa also declared in favour the vote was tied at 4–4. The committee debate went into extra time; first England and then Wales changed their minds, and the Rugby World Cup was born.

The first tournament was held in New Zealand and Australia in 1987. It was a 16-team invitational tournament and New Zealand won. The tournament has been held every four years since then but only really came alive in South Africa in 1995. Qualifying tournaments were introduced for the 1991 Rugby World Cup and they have helped to strengthen the game in the nations lower down the world rankings. By the time of the 2011 competition, 86 different nations took part in the early stages.

> ### *Did you know?*
>
> *When the World Cup comes to England in 2015, 2.9 million spectators are expected, including 400,000 overseas visitors. The global television audience is set to be over four billion, making this the third-largest sporting event in the world.*

The trophy stayed in the southern hemisphere for the first four competitions, perhaps explaining why those nations had been so keen on the idea. England secured the trophy for the first time with a drop goal from Jonny Wilkinson in the dying seconds of the final against Australia in Sydney in 2003.

The Barbarians

Often playing around the fringes of international competitions, there is one multi-national rugby club that defies normal sporting conventions and is more than a match for any national side. Formed in 1890 by William Percy Carpmael, the Barbarians were a side with no ground and no clubhouse. Membership was by invitation and the only qualification was that the player had to be of a high enough standard on the pitch and a decent chap off it. The dream was for the Barbarians to be an utterly cosmopolitan side spreading good fellowship among rugby players.

The Barbarians' early tours were around the UK, but in 1948 they were invited by the Home Nations to put together a side to play the visiting Australians. The Australians were keen to secure some additional gate receipts in order to fund an extension to their tour to play in Canada. The game, which the Barbarians won 9–6, proved to be such a success that a match against the Barbarians has been a highlight of subsequent tours ever since.

With players drawn from all over the world, the Barbarians have beaten all of the leading southern hemisphere sides at one point or another and enjoyed fixtures against the Home Nations, the British and Irish Lions and some of the lower-ranked rugby nations, such as Tunisia, Germany and Belgium. They pride themselves in playing open, free-running rugby and are always a delight to watch.

Barbarian fact file:

- *Players from 25 different countries have turned out for the Barbarians since 1890.*
- *The Barbarians arguably scored the best-ever try against the All Blacks in 1973 when the ball was carried from inside the Barbarians' 25-yard line, through seven pairs of hands, before Gareth Edwards scored under the posts.*
- *Tony O'Reilly of Old Belvedere and Ireland played 30 times for the club between 1955 and 1962 scoring a club record of 38 tries.*
- *The Barbarians' first tour consisted of games against Huddersfield and Bradford.*
- *There is no such country as Barbaria.*

In other international rugby news...

246 The number of points that the tiny island nation of Vanuatu has conceded in its five Rugby World Cup matches, while scoring just 40 points of their own. Vanuatu also holds the record for the most Rugby World Cup matches played without winning a single game.

152–0 The score when Paraguay lost to Argentina in May 2002, winning the record for the largest margin of defeat in an international fixture.

3 The number of points Chinese Taipei managed to score while conceding 155 to Japan in 2002.

14-5

The score as displayed using notches carved into a nearby tree when Samoa lost to Tonga in 1924. The international fixture was very nearly not covered in the *Samoa Times* because the rugby correspondent was at a hopscotch match instead. Fortunately one of the newspaper's compositors attended the rugby and reported the result. Before then Samoa played their first matches with empty coconut shells, until the New Zealand Rugby Union gave them a few balls in the early 1900s.

120

The number of rugby unions in different nations around the world at the time of writing.

101

The number of national teams competing against each other and ranked by the International Rugby Board at the time of writing. New Zealand on one side of the globe sits proudly at the top of those rankings for most of the time, and until a new country gets organised enough to play international rugby, Finland will probably sit just as proudly at the bottom.

THE PROFESSIONALS

When rugby union turned professional in 1995 it created a major upheaval in the game, especially in England. Until that point the major clubs competed in the Courage League but it was a fairly relaxed affair with the fixtures being organised on an adhoc basis between the clubs themselves. Professional sport meant a more professionally run Premiership with fixtures often planned to suit television schedules. Revenues were pooled, and arrangements made for a salary cap and a fixed maximum total wage bill for all clubs to allay the fears that an unbridled free market would unbalance the teams and destroy the competition.

The French, meanwhile, had an established senior-level club competition that had been around more or less since 1892. Players in the French Top 14 league also enjoyed a significantly higher salary cap than their English equivalents. The English rugby authorities attempted to stem the flow of top stars heading over the channel in search of higher wages by insisting that only those playing in domestic clubs would be eligible for selection to the national side. That hasn't stopped the likes of Jonny Wilkinson and others heading to the south of France after their international career has come to a natural end.

The top French clubs have stolen a march on the rest of the northern hemisphere in terms of investment, attendances and budgets. In the 2009–10 season the leading French club Toulouse enjoyed a €33-million budget, whereas Leicester, the wealthiest English club that season, could only rustle up €21 million. French clubs were allowed by the French National Rugby League to spend around €10 million on the players' wage bill, whereas the figure in England was roughly half that amount.

Filling the stands

 Attendance at top-level club rugby has increased, however, since the professional era began. The average crowd at a Premiership game in 1997–98 was around 6,000 but by 2010–11 that had increased to almost 12,000. Many clubs will also hold one or two special games a season where they slash the prices to attract a bigger crowd, and move their games to Twickenham or Wembley to accommodate them all.

As the international game has become more popular over recent decades, the opportunity to see the global stars playing throughout the season in club fixtures has no doubt helped to swell the crowds and the coffers of the top sides. A study by sports economists at University College Dublin, however, found that the main factor that affects attendance levels is simply how often the team wins at home. Regular home wins set the turnstiles spinning and so the financial rewards for the stronger home sides are significant and growing.

Even players in the lower leagues will occasionally benefit from the arrival of professionalism. Every so often a local side will find itself a wealthy benefactor prepared to pay players a token amount per game in an attempt to build a stronger club. Although many argue that the payments distort local leagues and divert money from investment in new facilities, for many young players the cash can be a very welcome source of additional income, and an incentive to train and play well.

Typical week of a Premiership rugby player

Monday

- *Swimming pool recovery session*
- *Medical screening for any injuries picked up at the weekend*
- *Match video analysis*
- *Light run out – touch rugby*

Tuesday

- *Contact rugby session – 75 per cent intensity*
- *Backs moves and kicking practice*
- *Set-piece training – line-outs and scrums*
- *Weight training*

Wednesday

- *Day off*

Thursday

- *Contact rugby session – 75 per cent intensity*
- *Backs moves and kicking practice*

- *Set-piece training – line-outs and scrums*
- *Weight training*

Friday

- *Team run – jogging through the planned plays with the team selected for the game*

Saturday

- *Light breakfast*
- *Walk through the moves for the day with the squad*
- *Primer session – stretches*
- *Light lunch three hours before kick-off*
- *Pre-match warm-up*
- *Final motivational team talks*
- *The game*
- *Ice bath*

Sunday

- *Day off*

Power packs

Tom Fordyce of BBC Sport has calculated the average weight and height of an England international forward over the past five decades:

YEAR	WEIGHT	HEIGHT
1962	92.5 kg	1.83 m
1972	97.75 kg	1.89 m
1982	89.9 kg	1.86 m
1992	106.5 kg	1.88 m
2002	110.1 kg	1.86 m
2012	112.9 kg	1.92 m

The management team

The back-room support behind a successful team can make the difference between winning and losing. As described in his book *Winning!*, head coach Clive Woodward assembled the following group that took the England national team to World Cup victory in 2003:

- Team manager
- Coach
- Assistant coach
- Assistant coach (kicking)
- Team doctor
- Team physiotherapist
- Team fitness advisor
- Scrummaging advisor
- Team masseur
- Video analyst
- Press officer
- Baggage master
- Referee advisor
- Head of performance services
- PA
- Media relations manager

TRAINING

*Throughout the week I have one side of me that does all the
preparation and resting and eating well and training, then it
hands all that over to the second individual, and that other
individual is a hugely competitive, instinctive one who is
just desperate to win. He is a bit of a monster, actually.*

JONNY WILKINSON, ENGLAND RUGBY PLAYER, *THE GUARDIAN*

For the casual player, training in rugby is by no means compulsory.
For those aiming for a place in the first team, it might be a good idea
to turn up and train once in a while to impress the selectors and to
remind them that you exist. However, there are plenty of second-,
third- and fourth-team captains who will happily give you a game,
regardless of whether you have made it to the midweek fitness and
drills session.

But building your strength, confidence and ball-handling skills will
always be useful come the weekend games. Training sessions are also
a good opportunity to learn from senior players some of the tricks,
techniques and set-piece moves that will make your 80 minutes of
competitive rugby on Saturday afternoons all the more enjoyable.

More importantly, training regularly with a rugby club is one of the best ways to improve your level of fitness and general well-being. For many people, training in a group is much more motivational than training on your own. There will probably be someone else close to your size and general fitness and skill level to work alongside.

Most community-based clubs will warmly welcome you at training on one or two evenings a week. Under floodlights for much of the year, amateur coaches will run prospective players through a series of warm-ups, stretches, fitness routines, drills and exercises to get you into the best possible shape to represent the club well.

The classic training grid

One of the most popular and common training drills is when the players line up on four corners of a square, approximately 5 m apart. Players will then, one at a time, run with a ball diagonally into the middle of the square and pass the ball to a player coming from the opposite corner.

Players have to keep their wits about them to dodge players running and passing at 90 degrees to their line while making sure that they catch the pass that is coming to them and deliver a sympathetic and easy-to-catch pass to the next person. Once the players have mastered this at a jogging pace, coaches will speed things up a bit or add new complications.

Players must concentrate on getting their hands ready in a position to accept a pass and communicate verbally and non-verbally with teammates in order to avoid the embarrassment of dropping a ball. After five or ten minutes, making short accurate passes becomes second nature.

Training kit

One thing to remember in training is that no one wants to get themselves injured unnecessarily. For that reason, a lot of club training sessions will involve large quantities of foam, in various shapes and sizes, wrapped up in brightly coloured waterproof vinyl. Tackle pads are used to allow players to train hard in simulated contact situations while reducing the knocks and injuries that might otherwise occur.

Touch rugby

Another great way of avoiding injuries at training is to play touch rugby. This is essentially the same as full-contact rugby except that a tackle is deemed to have been made when one player touches an opponent, ideally with two hands, on the hips, below the waistband. The tackled player then stops and heels the ball back to another teammate for play to continue.

As it takes the contact, rucks and mauls out of the game, touch rugby is a great way for players of all levels of ability within a team to get the ball in their hands and practise running at gaps, timing their moves, catching, passing and generally communicating better with other players.

Touch rugby has the added advantage that it can also be played all year round and in mixed teams, so the men's and the women's sides in a club can occasionally train together. Some clubs use it as a gentle introduction to the sport for new players, before persuading them to try the full-contact version.

Line-out moves

Training sessions are the perfect place to compose the complex series of code words and choreographed switches of position, dummy jumps and lifts that make up the modern line-out. When your side is awarded a line-out throw-in, every effort must be made to ensure that one of your own side catches the ball cleanly. The advantage lies in your teammates knowing where the ball is going to go and precisely when it is going to be thrown, and having a 'jumper' in the air at the right time in the right place.

Hours can be spent at the training pitch establishing new codes, signals, and ways to trick the opposition and hide your own side's intentions. At the very least, though, a basic code is required to signal whether the ball is going to be aimed at the front, middle or back of the line-out.

Hookers also need to put in a good few hours on the training pitch to be able to throw the oval ball in a perfectly straight line to a predictable height and length. Standing on the try line and aiming the ball at a fixed point on the goalposts will help the aspiring hooker to get their eye in. Varying the throwing distance from the goalpost from 5 m, 7 m and 9 m will simulate the conditions for a throw to the front, middle and back of the line.

The diet of champions

Nutrition is increasingly important for rugby players who want to get their bodies into the optimum physical condition for a game. A good diet provides the raw materials to build and repair muscles, as well as providing the energy to last the intense 80 minutes of a game. Top-level players will have a strictly controlled diet, personally tailored to their own body and playing position, but even the lowest-level amateur player can benefit from the professional rugby players' dietary tips.

Fluids

Getting enough liquid on board, in a form other than beer, is hugely important for rugby players. Top international players have been known to lose up to 3.5 kg in weight during a game, and that is almost entirely down to water loss. A lack of fluids leads to an immediate drop in performance. Advice given to the England squad in 2002 was that players should drink at least 3 litres a day and that a 3 per cent reduction in hydration would lead to a 10 per cent reduction in strength and an 8 per cent reduction in speed.

Carbohydrates

Carbohydrates provide energy for training and playing, and are absolutely essential for rugby players. Complex carbs are best because they release their energy slowly and steadily throughout the day; soybeans, sweet potatoes, lentils, apples, oranges, wholewheat pasta, brown rice, wholewheat bread, oats and fresh vegetables are good three hours before a game. Sugary refined carbs can be good after a game, once you have properly rehydrated, to get energy quickly back into the muscles.

It is important to match the calories going in with the energy that you expend. For the average British male, who now weighs around 83 kg (13 stone), 80 minutes of rugby burns off 1,089 calories. That is the equivalent of 6 pints of beer. Perfect for the post-match celebration in the clubhouse. In fact many clubs will happily sell you the beer in a 6-pint jug for your ease and convenience.

Protein

Protein is important for muscle repair and regrowth, and professional players will be advised to think about including protein with every meal. Eggs, lean meat, poultry and fish are all good. You should avoid processed meats such as pâté, salami and sausages, and anything that is deep-fried in batter. It is important to keep taking on protein even on rest days, as that is when the body builds new muscle.

Fat

The good news for rugby players is that not all fat is bad for you. You should of course avoid saturated fats (butter and lard) and trans-fats, which are formed when fats are fried, so burgers and fried food are pretty much out. Cold-water fish like salmon, trout, mackerel and sardines are packed full of oils that are so good for you they have been declared to be utterly 'essential'. Olive oil is also tremendously good for you, so much so that perhaps the traditional rugby song should be rewritten…

 Four and twenty bottles of extra virgin olive oil went down to Inverness…

Scrum machines

In the late 1970s Tim Francis, a teacher at Dulwich College in south London, had a little sideline making and selling exercise mats. His school had always had a strong rugby side and Francis began thinking about building a training machine that would allow the forwards to safely train for the increasingly technical aspects of scrummaging.

In the staff common room, he started to build experimental models out of cotton reels and matchsticks, before moving on to full-scale prototypes made from 200-litre drums and planks of wood. By 1980 he had given up the day job, moved to Devon and was working full time to create the Powerhouse, the first mass-produced and marketed scrum machine.

The first outing for the Powerhouse was at a Roslyn Park National Schools Sevens tournament in March 1982. The machine was left at the side of the pitches for teams to try out, in between games. By the end of the day Francis had orders for six machines and the business was up and running.

England prop Jeff Probyn, recalling an early scrum machine that he used at Bath University that used hydraulic pressure to simulate the forces an opposition pack might apply, said, 'The first time they released the pressure I was literally pushed through the back of my boots because the pressure split the seams.'

Today scrum machines have become much more sophisticated, with sensors and computers to calculate the combined forces being applied. As the laws about the scrum seem to change almost every season, the latest scrum machines even have alarms set to predict when the referee might blow up for an infringement.

CHAPTER 9

THE SPIRIT
OF RUGBY

A player must be ready to give and take hard knocks
but he will give and take them with a grin.
RUGGER, W. WAKEFIELD AND H. MARSHALL

At the end of many a game of rugby, players, spectators and commentators talk among themselves about the 'spirit' in which the game was played and whether or not it was the right one. A game played in the right spirit is one where the contest is uncompromising, tough, aggressive and physical, quite often played with a real anger and heartfelt loathing of your opposite number. However, immediately after the final whistle is blown, players on both sides will show the utmost respect, affection and genuine friendship towards their opponents. Indeed, the harder the game is played, the greater the degree of respect that is given.

The spirit of rugby draws heavily on the ancient codes of chivalry by which knights of old would do battle within a set of rules designed to ensure a fair fight. Victory would be sought not at all costs, but with honour. Much the same set of codes applies to rugby. There is an expectation that you will play with a certain degree of ferocity and animosity. To do less than that would in itself be disrespectful to your opponent. Whether you win or lose, a team that plays its rugby in the right spirit will be invited back year after year for another match.

Very rarely will you see a rugby player feign injury in order to trick a referee into punishing an opponent. Not for rugby the histrionics and Oscar-winning performances associated with the association game. More often than not a rugby player will keep quiet about any stray punch or shoeing that he or she might have received. Far better to keep an opponent on the pitch where you or your teammates can exact some sort of revenge than to see them sent off to the safety of the clubhouse and a warm bath.

Quite often too a player will accept, maybe not cheerfully but certainly stoically, any revenge that might be exacted upon them. Many a player will be heard to say that they probably deserved the shoeing or slap that followed a particular misdemeanour. The team captains resolved disputes in the very earliest games; today many a minor dispute is resolved between players without any need for a referee or assistant referee to get involved.

Rugby in literature

Perhaps it is not surprising that rugby, having been created in a seat of learning, should also inspire some great literature. The game of rugby itself has such a powerful narrative that it has led to some great reads.

Castle Gay – **John Buchan**

John Buchan may be better known for giving the world *The Thirty-Nine Steps*, but he also made a useful contribution to the rugby literary canon. Castle Gay is a tale of the self-discovery of a media mogul named Craw, overseen by Jaikie Galt, an international rugby player. They travel around the Scottish wilderness re-evaluating their lives and values and coming to differing conclusions.

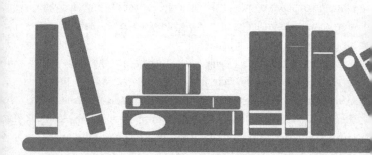

Tom Brown's School Days – **Thomas Hughes**

Thomas Hughes' semi-autobiographical novel of 1857 is set at Rugby School and was originally published as being written by 'an old boy of Rugby'. The character of Tom Brown is based on Hughes' brother George. Amid tales of bullying and cruelty, there is a description of Tom's early experience of finding himself at the bottom of a ruck in the middle of a game on the school playing fields. As the other players are hauled off him, Tom is discovered lying on the ground motionless and winded. As Tom gets his breath back and seems none the worse for wear, the older players conclude, 'Well, he is a plucky youngster, and will make a player.'

The Adventure of the Sussex Vampire – **Arthur Conan Doyle**

In this Sherlock Holmes tale published in 1924 we discover the key fact in Dr Watson's back-story that perhaps best describes his loyal, resourceful and determined nature. Watson previously played rugby for Blackheath.

A Story – **Dylan Thomas**

Thomas's tale of a young boy from west Wales travelling with a group of men on a drunken journey to Porthcawl contains a delightful gem of rugby-related dialogue, or what might have passed for banter in those days, between Enoch Davies and 'a stranger' who claims to have played for Aberavon in 1898. Davies calls him a liar; when the stranger says he can show him photos, Davies says they must be forged; when he offers to show him his cap, he says it must be stolen. Finally the stranger, furious, says he has friends to back him up. '"Bribed," said Enoch Davies.'

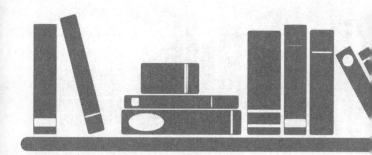

Work, Sex and Rugby – **Lewis Davies**

This book from 1998 describing one man's odyssey through a weekend of drinking, rugby and women was voted the best book to describe Wales by the World Book Day campaign to encourage more reading, particularly by young men.

How Green Was My Valley – **Richard Llewellyn**

Set in the mining village of Gilfach Goch near Tonypandy, Llewellyn's 1939 novel offers perhaps the most poetic description anywhere of what happens in Wales when a fly half fails to get rid of the ball quickly enough and, being greedy to score a try himself rather than pass to his wing, tries to sell a dummy to his opponent (Cyfartha): 'and how the crowd is laughing now, for to sell a dummy to Cyfartha is to sell poison to a Borgia…'

The music of rugby

Part of the warm-up ritual for supporters and players alike is a little clearing of the windpipes and a spot of communal singing. Rugby has become associated with some great anthems and has inspired composers to pen a few more tunes.

'Rugby (Symphonic Movement No. 2)' – Arthur Honegger, 1928

The Swiss composer, born in France, was inspired to produce his second symphonic movement while watching the rugby in the Colombes stadium in Paris, home of the Racing Metro rugby club.

> *I very much like the game of football, but I prefer rugby. I find it more spontaneous, more direct and closer to nature than football, which is a more scientific game. For me the savage, brusque, untidy and desperate rhythm of rugby is more attractive.*

'Swing Low, Sweet Chariot'– Wallace Willis, c.1909

It was of course those public school boys who would give English rugby its finest anthem. In the last game of the 1988 season, a group of boys from the Benedictine Douai School in Woolhampton, Berkshire, were at Twickenham to watch the game against Ireland. Under the guidance of Benedictine monks the school's first XV had adopted the hymn 'Swing Low, Sweet Chariot', and the schoolboys began to sing their team song from the stands. Nigerian-born winger Chris Oti was having a great game that day and the schoolboys sang with particular enthusiasm each time he got the ball. In the end Oti had run in a hat-trick of tries and the England supporters had a new anthem that would travel the world with them.

'Cwm Rhondda' – John Hughes, 1905

Also known as the 'Welsh Rugby Hymn', 'Cwm Rhondda' is the tune written by John Hughes used as a setting for the words of William Williams' 'Guide Me, O Thou Great Redeemer'. Sung whenever Wales are playing, it is one of the few tunes where the terrace choirs split into two parts, with one section repeating the last three syllables of the penultimate line of each verse. The tradition of Welsh male-voice choirs means this is almost always the most tunefully rendered anthem at any rugby fixture. Annoyingly, football fans have stolen the music for their own, somewhat less elegant chant, 'You're not singing any more'.

'World in Union' – lyrics by Charlie Skarbek, 1991

This probably was commissioned, no doubt with the best of intentions, by a committee of the International Rugby Board. It borrows the tune from the powerful and moving hymn 'I Vow to Thee My Country', which in turn borrows its tune from Holst's 'Jupiter' from 'The Planets'. Skarbek makes a brave but not entirely successful attempt with his lyrics to capture the spirit of international friendship that pervades rugby union. To be honest, it is only brought out every four years at the World Cup, listened to politely at the opening ceremony and then quietly forgotten once the proper community singing and Haka takes over.

The Haka

The pre-match ritual of a traditional warlike chant, with accompanying chest beating, thigh slapping and exaggerated facial gestures performed by the New Zealand national rugby team goes back to their very first international tour. Before their own national rugby union had been formally constituted, a Maori team was assembled, packed off on a steamer and arrived at Tilbury Docks in England on 27 September 1888. Wearing traditional capes, they performed a Haka before their first game against a scratch Surrey XV, which they then went on to win 4–1.

In 1905 the first All Blacks team to tour Britain, known as 'the Originals', performed the now popular 'Ka Mate' Haka before their Welsh test and the *West Coast Times* reported that, 'The crowd listened and watched in pleased silence, and thundered their approval at its close.'

The Haka has not always been so popular with opposition teams obliged to stand and respectfully watch the New Zealand side pump themselves up while directing hostile gestures at them before a game. Various international sides have responded to the Haka in different ways with varying degrees of success. The Irish side of 1989 linked arms and, led by captain and lock Willie Anderson, edged forwards during the performance until they were almost nose-to-nose with the All Blacks team. In 2008 the Welsh stood motionless after the Haka, leading to a two-minute stare-off with the Kiwis, and ignoring the referee's pleas for them to begin the game.

Legendary Irish centre Brian O'Driscoll was accused of disrespecting the Kiwi tradition, however, when he picked up a piece of grass and threw it in the air in a gesture symbolising the picking up of a white feather. A few minutes into the test, O'Driscoll was spear-tackled by the New Zealand captain Tana Umaga, dislocating the Irish centre's shoulder and putting him out of the game and the rest of the tour.

At Cardiff Arms Park in 1905, in response to the All Blacks' Haka, the Welsh players led the massed terraces in a powerful rendition of 'Land of My Fathers' and inspired a heroic victory over the New Zealanders. No one would suggest that the impartial referee would have been influenced by the intimidating atmosphere in the stadium, but an apparent late try by Kiwi centre Bob Deans was ruled to have been held up in a tackle and not scored. The power of pre-match Welsh voices lifted in praise of the Almighty who does, we are told, move in mysterious ways.

For all its bravado and symbolism, the intimidating chant is thought to be linked to the story of a Maori warrior Te Rauparaha who, running away to escape his enemies, hides in a storage pit. Emerging blinking into the sunlight he sees a friendly chief, known as Te Wharerangi ('the hairy man'). It's really not that terrifying when you think about it.

> *Ka mate, ka mate*
> *Ka ora, ka ora*
> *Tenei te tangata puhuruhuru*
> *Nana i tiki mai whakawhiti te ra*
> *Upane, upane*
> *Upane kaupane*
> *Whiti te ra.*

These words are translated as:

> *It is death, it is death*
> *It is life, it is life*
> *This is the hairy man*
> *Who caused the sun to shine again for me*
> *Up the ladder, up the ladder*
> *Up to the top*
> *The sun shines.*

New Zealanders do not have a monopoly on pre-rugby war-dance rituals. The Tongans, Fijians and Samoans have their own Hakas to help fire up their players and intimidate the opposition. The English have yet to pluck up the courage to begin all their international fixtures by celebrating the traditional cultural art form that is the morris dance. Perhaps one day?

Rugby reaches war-torn Rwanda

In 1994 Rwanda was devastated by one of the most horrific acts of genocide, when 800,000 people were killed over 100 days of violence between Hutus and Tutsis. After a slow period of reconciliation and reconstruction a number of international development organisations began to work there to help rebuild the nation.

One such organisation was Voluntary Service Overseas, and one volunteer in 2001 was Emma Rees, an international politics graduate and keen rugby player from Aberystwyth University. On her own as an English teacher in a solely French-speaking village, Emma found settling in initially quite difficult as her French was limited. She also missed playing rugby and so, with one rugby ball and a few coloured socks filled with sand to mark out a playing area, Emma introduced her pupils to the game.

At first, when she showed them a video of a rather tough Cardiff game the children were terrified. However, Rwanda is known as the land of a thousand hills so their natural fitness levels were very high. Emma convinced them to play and they loved it. The game spread quickly among the local children and Emma formed the Federation of Rwandan Rugby to develop the sport. A charity, Friends of Rwandan Rugby, was created shortly afterwards, with rugby legends like Jason Leonard among its patrons. Over the years numerous coaches and players from overseas have travelled to Rwanda to help spread word of the game and help young people make new friends through the sport.

Rwanda is now an associate member of the International Rugby Board and in 2010 its national side, the Silverbacks, beat Burundi 39–13. They regularly travel to compete in the Hong Kong Tens competition. Thanks to one rugby-mad girl from Aberystwyth, the game continues to grow and create new friendships all around the world.

CHAPTER 10

GREAT STADIUMS, GREAT GAMES

*The players' changing room at Twickenham
was as inspiring as a prison cell.*

CLIVE WOODWARD, ENGLAND NATIONAL COACH, IN *WINNING!*

As the game of rugby grew in popularity, bigger and better stadiums were needed. International rugby unions have found the resources to create spectacular settings on which to stage some very special sporting moments and the supporters, with their own particular approach to the art of spectating, have also played their part in making the game what it is today.

Unlike the association game, with segregated stands and the ever-present threat of violence breaking out on the terraces and sometimes even on to the pitch, rugby terraces have tended to be far more affable environments. Fans of opposing sides are seated together and might engage in a little good-natured banter, but rarely anything more serious. Fans are also mostly trusted to enjoy an alcoholic drink or two as they watch the game.

For many, the rituals of the journey to the stadium are as important as the game itself: the pre-match breakfast, the train or car journey to the ground, a pint or two nearby and a spot of lunch, and the final walk to the stadium with fellow fans as the atmosphere builds.

Twickenham Stadium, London

- *Formerly a market garden that was purchased by the RFU in 1907 for £5,572 12s 6d.*
- *Still referred to as Billy's Cabbage Patch after Billy Williams, the RFU committee member who made the original investment.*
- *Opened in 1909 and has been the English rugby team's headquarters ever since.*
- *The South Stand was demolished in 2005 and rebuilt, increasing the total capacity to 82,000.*
- *Stage for the first streaker, Michael O'Brien, to bare all in front of thousands at a sporting event during an England v Wales fixture in 1974.*

Murrayfield Stadium, Edinburgh

- *Largest sports arena of any sort in Scotland.*
- *Home to the Scottish national side and the Edinburgh club side since March 1925.*
- *Hosted its biggest crowd when 104,000 fans watched Scotland play Wales.*
- *Modern all-seating capacity now 67,130.*
- *Scene of one of the worst-ever opening sequences for Scotland when Italy scored 21 points against them in just five minutes in 2007.*

Ellis Park Stadium, Johannesburg

- *Home to the Springboks since 1928.*
- *Host to the 1995 Rugby World Cup final.*
- *Host to the first-ever rugby international to require a period of extra time (South Africa v New Zealand).*
- *The original ground was rebuilt in 1979–80.*
- *Listed on the London Stock Exchange in 1987.*

Millennium Stadium, Cardiff

- *Opened in time for the millennium celebrations.*
- *Shared with the Welsh national football team.*
- *Has a fully retractable roof and a capacity of 74,500.*
- *The stage for Wales' biggest-ever win (30–3) over England, in 2013, crushing English hopes of a Grand Slam and winning the Six Nations tournament.*

Stade de France, Paris

- *Built for the 1998 FIFA World Cup and used by the national football and rugby teams.*
- *Capacity of 81,338.*
- *The only stadium in the world to have hosted a Rugby World Cup final and the association game.*
- *The French didn't get to play in the 2007 Rugby World Cup final in their nation's capital, having been knocked out by England in the semis.*

Stadium Australia, Sydney

- *Built for the Olympics in 2000.*
- *Squeezed in some six-figure crowds for a few fixtures before whittling its capacity down to 83,500.*
- *Has the unusual ability to morph from a rectangular pitch for rugby union, rugby league and the occasional football match into an oval one for playing Aussie rules.*
- *Hosted the final and deciding test of the Irish and British Lions tour in 2013, which the Lions won by 41–16.*

CHAPTER 11

RUGBY FOR ALL

*Rugby is… a universal sport that can be enjoyed
by anyone with some space and a ball.*

KATE PORTER, AUSTRALIAN RUGBY PLAYER

Rugby takes great pride in being a game that everyone can play. It is a game played by men and women, and it keeps evolving, with new versions of the sport springing up all the time. The same principles remain throughout each variety as it seeks to find more ways to allow people to enjoy picking up a ball and running with it.

The full-contact version of rugby is safer and more enjoyable if there is soft ground and rich turf to fall on, and that means that during the warmer months of the year when the ground is harder there is less rugby to be found. Former All Blacks player, diplomat and Member of the New Zealand Parliament Chris Laidlaw said that, 'Rugby may have many problems, but the gravest is undoubtedly that of the persistence of summer.' So a number of new versions of the sport have been developed precisely to get around that particular concern. Other adaptations have been made to allow wheelchair users to enjoy a version of the sport and one special game has been created just for the backs.

Rugby Sevens

Sevens is played during the summer on a full-sized pitch, with two halves of just seven minutes each, the scrums consisting of just three players from each side. With fewer players, there is a lot more running around. Some people have suggested that the main reason for organising Sevens tournaments is to give the backs a chance to run about and warm up after a long season standing around in the cold waiting for the forwards to release the ball.

With the shorter games and typical tournament format, Sevens festivals lend themselves to a lot of drinking. The Hong Kong Sevens is the premier international competition, played in March every year, as 24 teams compete over three days for a prize fund of US$150,000. The atmosphere in the South Stand of the Hong Kong Stadium can get very lively, with fancy dress, Mexican waves and the inevitable streakers. The London Sevens fills up Twickenham Stadium for two days each May, with an equally colourful display of costumes and alcohol-fuelled antics in and around the games.

Beach rugby

Hot on the heels of beach volleyball, a new seaside sporting spectacle is emerging. Swansea has hosted an annual beach rugby tournament since 2006 and in 2010 it attracted 30 teams and a crowd of over 2,500. International tournaments have also been organised in Italy and France.

Myles Ward, an enterprising young wine dealer, found that he and his friends enjoyed a holiday beach rugby tournament in France so much, that in 2013 he decided to reserve a corner of the Covent Garden Piazza in London, order a few lorry loads of sand, find a brewer to sponsor the proceedings, and created the first London Beach Rugby tournament.

The pitch for the inaugural London Beach Rugby tournament measured 25 m x 15 m and was surrounded by an inflatable wall. The game is played on a touch-rugby basis, with each side allowed to take three tackles before the ball is turned over to the other side. Two halves of seven minutes each are played with five players on each side and rolling substitutions.

Rugby netball

The Rugby Netball League was established in 1907 and is played on Clapham Common in south London during the summer. As the name suggests, scoring involves dropping the ball into a net at either end of the pitch. Players can pass in any direction and there are no offside laws. The pace is frenetic and, with a sun-baked pitch, the tackles can be extremely hard.

Time Out described it as a 'bizarre hybrid of a sport', and with its huge nets, measuring around 1 m across and suspended 3.5 m in the air, Mike Bushell of BBC Sport called it 'netball for giants'.

Wheelchair rugby

Rugby also takes great pride in the diversity of its players and the wide range of abilities that flourish on the pitch. This Paralympic sport was created in 1976 by a group of Canadian wheelchair athletes. Originally called 'murderball' because of its aggressive, full-contact nature, the game was essentially a spiced-up version of wheelchair basketball.

Played on a hardwood court the same size as a basketball court, players score by carrying the ball over the goal line but their opponents can use their wheelchairs to block and stop them. It is a fast-moving game, as players must pass or bounce the ball within ten seconds. More than 24 countries play the sport and it became a Paralympic sport in Sydney in 2000, with the USA taking home the first gold medal.

Mark Zupan, who captained the US team in 2004, said,

> *Breaking my neck was the best thing that ever happened to me. I have an Olympic medal. I've been to so many countries I would never have been, met so many people I would never have met. I've done more in the chair... than a whole hell of a lot of people who aren't in chairs.*

Why every rugby ground matters

Although its national side might not always come out on top, England wins when it comes to sheer numbers of people who take part in the sport. In the nation where the game was invented there are over 1,800 clubs and just short of two million players. Whether they are pre-teens running around on a Sunday morning or gentlemen moving into late middle age, still keeping up their club membership so that they can enter the ballot for international tickets, they are all part of a vast, extended rugby family.

While England does well for the numbers of players it manages to report to the statisticians at the International Rugby Board, New Zealand leads the world in terms of the number of rugby clubs per capita. For every 100,000 people the Kiwis somehow manage to sustain 14 rugby clubs. In England, for every 100,000 people there are on average only two rugby clubs.

Nation	Clubs	Players
England	1,089	1,990,988
Wales	314	79,800
Scotland	257	217,057
Ireland	234	153,823
New Zealand	600	146,893
Australia	767	297,389
South Africa	1,526	320,842
France	1,798	360,847

Population	Players per 1,000 population	Clubs per 100,000 population
53,010,000	38	2
3,064,000	26	10
5,295,000	41	5
4,589,000	34	5
4,433,000	33	14
22,680,000	13	3
51,190,000	6	3
65,700,000	5	3

CHAPTER 12

A CALL
TO ARMS

*The women and men who play on that rugby field are
more alive than too many of us will ever be.*

VICTOR L. CAHN, PROFESSOR AND PLAYWRIGHT

Every year, rugby puts on a great display of international sportsmanship. With phenomenal games played by magnificent athletes in packed stadiums, rugby gives some of the best sporting entertainment in the world.

The benefits to wider society are huge. With over a hundred nations now playing the game, its power to strengthen international friendships is well recognised. As more and more people discover its joys every year, rugby is set to continue to go from strength to strength.

It is a simple game that can be appreciated from the safety of the sofa or the stands without any need for a huge degree of technical understanding. With a little more knowledge it can become a richer experience, and those who take up the opportunity to play it gain an even greater enjoyment of the strategies and tactics employed by the best sides.

In some cases, rugby has grown to become more than just a sport. Where there is a rugby club there are people who come together to play a game but often end up forming a community. The people who support each other physically on the pitch are the same people who support each other socially, emotionally and occasionally commercially off the pitch. The extended rugby family is a strong one and it sticks together.

For rugby to continue to grow and spread more joy around the world it needs players, supporters and volunteers. If you are a parent then you might want to think about dropping your little darlings off at a nearby rugby club on a Sunday morning, assuming of course that they run a mini or junior rugby section. This has the added advantage of giving you an hour or so uninterrupted with the Sunday papers. You might even find a degree of enjoyment supporting them from the touchline. If you get really keen, well, the world is your oyster. Rugby will always welcome those who are willing to pull on some boots, pick up a tackle bag and allow themselves to be run at and occasionally knocked over by small boys and girls carrying a rugby ball.

If you are already involved with a rugby club and worrying about the shortage of volunteers, don't worry, help is already at hand. A report by rugby sponsors Zurich found that 51 per cent of English former players would volunteer at their local rugby club if only someone had asked them. Rugby retains a loyal family of enthusiasts ready to pick up a tackle bag and coach and support the next generation of players.

Rugby clubs have grown over the years as people have made time for the simple but necessary tasks needed to keep them ticking over: filling in forms, sending off emails, remembering to bring a first-aid kit. Rugby clubs have thrived when one or two enthusiastic types have gone to the trouble of creating a team from scratch and setting up a few more fixtures.

So the next time you are making a new year's resolution to lose some weight, get fit or just get out more, why not point your new-found motivation and drive towards your nearest local rugby club. The Olympic movement has shown how powerful volunteering can be at multiplying the enjoyment, as well as the economic and social legacy, from major sporting events. Rugby, too, will benefit in the future if it taps into that spirit.

Rugby is a game to be played as well as watched and there are plenty of team captains and coaches all around the world looking for an extra player or two to make sure that they have a full side to play on Saturday. It will be easy to come up with one or two reasons why you shouldn't play: lack of fitness, lack of ability, lack of time or lack of boots. But there are many more reasons why you should play.

CONCLUSION

So, to end this little book about *The Joy of Rugby* here are just a selection of the many reasons why you should not only continue to enjoy following and watching this fine sport, but why you should find a pair of boots and, if at all possible, keep playing until the great referee upstairs blows the final whistle.

1. Rugby is a far better way of keeping fit and is much cheaper than going to the gym. Other people talk to you and you have to keep working out until the referee blows the final whistle.

2. People who play team sports are actually, and this has been scientifically proven, happier than other people.

3. In rugby this happiness might be something to do with the pre- and post-match huddle. When else can you get a hug from 15 people all at the same time?

4. Rugby is far better than football because no one wastes time arguing with referees or writhing around on the floor in fake agony whenever another player gets anywhere near them.

5. Rugby supporters can generally be trusted to drink before, during and after a game without necessarily causing a major riot.

6. Rugby is a total body workout combining cardiovascular effort running around in the backs and muscle-building strength work in the forwards.

7. Rugby players have been sharing the joys of a hot tub since well before they became a feature of expensive spas and health retreats.

8. Mud is extremely good for your complexion.

9. Rugby gives you the perfect excuse to enjoy the sinus-clearing, skin-tingling benefits of Deep Heat, Tiger Balm or Ralgex.

10. Being a member of a rugby club gets you into a ballot for tickets for the internationals.

11. Half-time oranges are delicious.

12. So are half-time glasses of port.

13. Playing in the scrum means that you have slightly more idea of what is going on when watching it being done professionally.

14. Playing in the front row of the scrum often means that your facial features can be used to frighten and discipline small children.

15. Cauliflower ears can be counted as one of your five a day.

16. You have an excuse for a romantic trip to Paris or Rome once every other year during the Six Nations.

17. You can enjoy a spot of communal singing without having to listen to a long sermon in church first.

18. Play rugby over a few years and you will inevitably pick up quite a lot of 'stash', and the rugby shirt is a style classic that never goes out of fashion.

19. You can enter a boat race (post-match drinking game) without having to go to Oxford or Cambridge.

20. If you drop a pass or fail to pick up a bouncing ball you can always blame the odd shape rather than your own incompetence.

21. Playing rugby will give you a group of friends for life.

22. No matter what shape or size you are there will always be a place for you somewhere in a rugby team.

23. If none of those reasons appeal, you could always become a referee.

ACKNOWLEDGEMENTS

Huge thanks are due to my editors Jen Barclay, Emily Kearns and Sophie Martin, who have done tremendous work knocking this book into shape, and to all the rugby bloggers and writers for sharing their thoughts and insights about this great game. In particular, I'd like to thank and recommend www.rugbyfootballhistory.com for its wonderfully curated archive of the sport and Dan Cottrell's www.betterrugbycoaching.com for anyone who wants to take their game even further.

PAUL OWEN

THE JOY OF RUNNING

Paul Owen

ISBN: 978 1 84953 458 1   Hardback   £9.99

Every day is a good day when you run.
KEVIN NELSON

This pocket-sized miscellany, packed with fascinating facts, handy hints and captivating stories and quotes from the world of running, is perfect for anyone who knows the joy of hitting the road.

THE JOY OF

GOLF

RAY HAMILTON

THE JOY OF GOLF

Ray Hamilton

ISBN: 978 1 84953 598 4   Hardback   £9.99

> *I don't play too much golf.*
> *Two rounds a day are plenty.*
> HARRY VARDON

This pocket-sized miscellany, packed with fascinating facts, handy hints and captivating stories and quotes from the world of golf, is perfect for anyone who knows the incomparable joy of hitting the fairway.

My Life as a
Hooker
When a Middle-Aged Bloke
Discovered Rugby

'If this is what a midlife crisis does for you, I want one.'
Luke Benedict, rugby writer for the *Daily Mail*

Steven Gauge

MY LIFE AS A HOOKER
When a Middle-Aged Bloke Discovered Rugby

Steven Gauge

ISBN: 978 1 84953 211 2   £7.99   Paperback

In my late thirties, it gradually dawned on me that I had become Jason's regular hooker. It was an arrangement that worked well for a couple of reasons. He didn't need me to dress up in anything particularly risqué or to do anything too vulgar, other than cuddle in the middle of a field with him and thirteen other men on a Saturday afternoon.

Steven Gauge's response to an impending midlife crisis didn't involve piercings, tattoos or a red sports car – instead, he decided to take up rugby. What he found on the pitch was a wonderful game, far removed from the professional televised glamour of international rugby, where ordinary blokes with ordinary jobs (and some extraordinary bellies) get together once in a while and have a great time rolling around in the mud.
By the end of his first few seasons, Steven had cracked his nose and various other parts of his anatomy – but he had cracked the game too, and found a place in the club as Captain of the Fourths.

'Steven Gauge writes with charm, wit and intelligence and real insight.'

Samira Ahmed, journalist and broadcaster

If you're interested in finding out more about our books, find us on Facebook at **Summersdale Publishers** and follow us on Twitter at **@Summersdale**.

www.summersdale.com